First World War
and Army of Occupation
War Diary
France, Belgium and Germany

59 DIVISION
Divisional Troops
470 Field Company Royal Engineers
24 February 1917 - 16 July 1919

WO95/3017/6

The Naval & Military Press Ltd
www.nmarchive.com
Published in association with The National Archives

Published by

The Naval & Military Press Ltd

Unit 10 Ridgewood Industrial Park,

Uckfield, East Sussex,

TN22 5QE England

Tel: +44 (0) 1825 749494

www.naval-military-press.com

www.nmarchive.com

This diary has been reprinted in facsimile from the original. Any imperfections are inevitably reproduced and the quality may fall short of modern type and cartographic standards.

© Crown Copyright
Images reproduced by permission of The National Archives, London, England, 2015.

Contents

Document type	Place/Title	Date From	Date To
Heading	WO95/3017/6 March 1919 Missing		
Heading	59th Division 470th Field Coy R.E. Feb 1917-July1919		
War Diary	Lark Hill Camp	24/02/1917	24/02/1917
War Diary	Salisbury Plain	24/02/1917	24/02/1917
War Diary	Havre	26/02/1917	27/02/1917
War Diary	Longueveau	28/02/1917	28/02/1917
War Diary	Blangy Trouville	01/03/1917	01/03/1917
War Diary	Warfuse-Abancourt	02/03/1917	09/03/1917
War Diary	Foucaucourt	10/03/1917	18/03/1917
War Diary	St. Christ	19/03/1917	19/03/1917
War Diary	Foucaucourt	20/03/1917	21/03/1917
War Diary	St Christ	22/03/1917	31/03/1917
Heading	To O A G 3rd Echelon Base		
War Diary	Blangy-Trouville	01/03/1917	01/03/1917
War Diary	Warfusee-Abancourt	04/03/1917	09/03/1917
War Diary	Foucaucourt	10/03/1917	18/03/1917
War Diary	St. Christ	19/03/1917	19/03/1917
War Diary	Foucaucourt	20/03/1917	21/03/1917
War Diary	St Christ	22/03/1917	02/04/1917
War Diary	Eterpigny	03/04/1917	06/04/1917
War Diary	Bouvincourt	07/04/1917	29/05/1917
War Diary	Metz-EN-Couture	30/05/1917	06/07/1917
War Diary	Le Mesnil-En-Arrouaise	09/07/1917	15/08/1917
War Diary	Le Transloy	15/08/1917	23/08/1917
War Diary	Bouzincourt	24/08/1917	01/09/1917
War Diary	Oudezeele	02/09/1917	10/09/1917
War Diary	Winnezeele	11/09/1917	14/09/1917
War Diary	Watou	20/09/1917	22/09/1917
War Diary	Ypres	24/09/1917	30/09/1917
War Diary	Vlamertinghe Seaton Camp	01/10/1917	03/10/1917
War Diary	La Lovie	04/10/1917	04/10/1917
War Diary	Boeseghem	05/10/1917	05/10/1917
War Diary	Delette	05/10/1917	10/10/1917
War Diary	Bailleul	11/10/1917	11/10/1917
War Diary	Hestrus	12/10/1917	13/10/1917
War Diary	Barlin	14/10/1917	14/10/1917
War Diary	Carency	15/10/1917	18/11/1917
War Diary	Gouy-En-Artois	19/11/1917	19/11/1917
War Diary	Blarville	20/11/1917	22/11/1917
War Diary	Equancourt	23/11/1917	24/11/1917
War Diary	Gouzeacourt	25/11/1917	27/11/1917
War Diary	Equancourt	27/11/1917	02/12/1917
War Diary	Ytres	03/12/1917	06/12/1917
War Diary	Trescault	07/12/1917	09/12/1917
War Diary	Flesquieres	10/12/1917	22/12/1917
War Diary	Beaulincourt	22/12/1917	25/12/1917
War Diary	Moncheaux	25/12/1917	08/02/1918
War Diary	Barly	09/02/1918	12/02/1918
War Diary	Mercatel	12/02/1918	12/02/1918
War Diary	St Leger	12/02/1918	28/02/1918

Heading	War Diary Of 59th Divisional Engineers War Diary 470th (N.M) Field Company R.E. March 1918		
War Diary	St Leger	01/03/1918	10/03/1918
War Diary	Noreuil	11/03/1918	21/03/1918
War Diary	Ayette	21/03/1918	22/03/1918
War Diary	Bouzincourt	23/03/1918	23/03/1918
War Diary	Pont Noyelles	25/03/1918	25/03/1918
War Diary	Montrelet	27/03/1918	28/03/1918
War Diary	Hermin	30/03/1918	31/03/1918
Heading	War Diary Of 59th Divisional Engineers 470th Field Company R.E. April 1918		
War Diary	Hermaville	01/04/1918	03/04/1918
War Diary	Watou	04/04/1918	07/04/1918
War Diary	St Jean Ypres	08/04/1918	12/04/1918
War Diary	Locre	13/04/1918	13/04/1918
War Diary	Kemmel	13/04/1918	21/04/1918
War Diary	Houtkerque	21/04/1918	27/04/1918
War Diary	St Jans-Ter-Biezen	28/04/1918	05/05/1918
War Diary	Houtkerque	06/05/1918	06/05/1918
War Diary	Stomer	07/05/1918	08/05/1918
War Diary	Rebecq	09/05/1918	09/05/1918
War Diary	Bours	10/05/1918	10/05/1918
War Diary	Dieval	11/05/1918	11/05/1918
War Diary	Maignil Le Ruits	12/05/1918	31/05/1918
War Diary	Bois-De-Olhain	01/06/1918	10/06/1918
War Diary	Calers Predefin Crepy	01/07/1918	24/07/1918
War Diary	Houdain	10/07/1918	15/07/1918
War Diary	Predefin	23/07/1918	23/07/1918
War Diary	Bellacourt	24/07/1918	26/08/1918
War Diary	Robecq	27/08/1918	31/08/1918
War Diary	Calonne	01/09/1918	03/09/1918
War Diary	Lestrem	04/09/1918	30/09/1918
Heading	1st Div. C.R.E. Field Cov Signals October 1918		
War Diary	Lestrem	01/10/1918	03/10/1918
War Diary	Fleurbaix	04/10/1918	18/10/1918
War Diary	Marquette	18/10/1918	19/10/1918
War Diary	Templeuve	20/10/1918	24/10/1918
War Diary	Toufflers	24/10/1918	09/11/1918
War Diary	Obigies	09/11/1918	12/11/1918
War Diary	Lewze	12/11/1918	18/11/1918
War Diary	Kain	18/11/1918	18/11/1918
War Diary	Templeuve	19/11/1918	19/11/1918
War Diary	Petit Ronchin	20/11/1918	03/12/1918
War Diary	Vaudricourt	04/12/1918	31/01/1919
Heading	D A G 329 Echelon War Diary		
War Diary	Vaudricourt	01/02/1919	01/02/1919
War Diary	Etaples	01/02/1919	28/02/1919
Heading	To G.O.C. British Troops 727 War Diary		
War Diary	Etaples	01/04/1919	30/04/1919
War Diary	Dunkirk	01/05/1919	31/05/1919
War Diary	Mardycke Camp Dunkirk	01/06/1919	16/07/1919
War Diary	Dunkirk	01/06/1919	16/07/1919

WO95
3017/6.

March 1919 missing

59TH DIVISION

470TH FIELD COY R.E.
FEB 1917-~~DEC 1918~~
July 1919

DUPLICATE

Army Form C. 2118.

WAR DIARY
or
INTELLIGENCE SUMMARY

470th Field Co. R.E.

Feb. 1917

(Erase heading not required.)

Place	Date	Hour	Summary of Events and Information	Remarks and references to Appendices
LARK HILL Camp, SALISBURY Plain	24/2/17	9.a.m.	Unit left AMESBURY Station in 2 train loads. Arrived at SOUTHAMPTON and embarked in S.S. ARCHIMEDES	
HAVRE	26/2/17	6.0 a.m.	Unit disembarked at HAVRE and marched to No 5. Docks Rest Camp.	
HAVRE	27/2/17	10.0 a.m.	Unit entrained at GARE des MACHANDISES	
LONGUEVEAU	28/2/17	1.0 a.m	Unit detrained and marched to QUSY — BLANGY—TRONVILLE where Unit stopped night in billets.	

Parker
Major & O.C.

470th (NORTH MIDLAND) FIELD COY.
R.E.

Copy DUPLICATE

Army Form C. 2118.

WAR DIARY
or
INTELLIGENCE SUMMARY.
(Erase heading not required.)

470. Field Co R.E

March 1917

Instructions regarding War Diaries and Intelligence Summaries are contained in F.S. Regs., Part II. and the Staff Manual respectively. Title pages will be prepared in manuscript.

Hour, Date, Place	Summary of Events and Information	Remarks and references to Appendices
5.0 am 1/3/17 BLANGY-TROUVILLE	Unit marched from BLANGY-TROUVILLE to WARFUSEE-ABANCOURT and was quartered in huts.	
9 am 2/3/17 WARFUSE-ABANCOUR	O.C. and 35 men left for FOUCAUCOURT to arrange for taking over from 4th Field Co R.E.	
11.0 am 4/3/17 "	Inspection by Brigadier General Tebreibe C.E. 3rd Corps.	
8.0 am 6/3/17 "	1 Officer 13 O.R. No 3 Section left for VAIRE-SOUS-CORBIE for work at Divisional School	
9.0 am 8/3/17 "	Remainder of No 3 Section left for VAIRE-SOUS-CORBIE and attached to H.Q. 72 Army Field Artillery Brigade	
8.30 am 9/3/17 "	Rest of Unit proceeded to FOUCAUCOURT and was quartered at CIMETIERE Camp.	
8.0 am 10/3/17 FOUCAUCOURT to 18/3/17	Unit engaged in reserve area on trenching, roads, and water supply.	
8.0 am 19/3/17 ST. CHRIST	Sections 1 and 4 proceeded to ST. CHRIST made footbridge and commenced road bridge across SOMME river and canal at ST. CHRIST	
8.0 am 20/3/17 FOUCAUCOURT	Section 3 returned from VAIRE-SOUS-CORBIE to FOUCAUCOURT	
9.0 am 21/3/17 "	Unit proceeded to ST. CHRIST	
8.0 am 22/3/17 ST. CHRIST	Bridge for Infantry and M. Line transport made across SOMME river and canal. Transport passed over ca. 1.0 pm 22/3/17	
5.0 am "	Heavy timber trestle bridge made across SOMME canal at ST. CHRIST	

DUPLICATE

Army Form C. 2118.

WAR DIARY
or
INTELLIGENCE SUMMARY.

(Erase heading not required.)

470. Field. Co. R.E.

March 1917

Hour, Date, Place	Summary of Events and Information	Remarks and references to Appendices
8.0 am. 22/3/17. ST CHRIST. to 27/3/17	Unit engaged on improving bridges and approaches and in order repairs VILLIERS— CARBONNEL — HAPPINCOURT — BRIOST — ST CHRIST — TROY — ENNERMAIN — ATHIES.	
8.0 am. 23/3/17 "	Bridge constructed across OMIGNON river at ST CHRIST	
8.0 am 25/3/17 "	Service trestle bridge placed across OMIGNON river at ATHIES Passage made round crater at ENNERMAIN	
8.0 am 27/3/17 to 31/3/17. "	Heavy timber trestle bridge made at ATHIES to replace service trestle bridge.	

JR Nader
Major R.E.
O.C.

Instructions regarding War Diaries and Intelligence Summaries are contained in F.S. Regs., Part II. and the Staff Manual respectively. Title pages will be prepared in manuscript.

To
D.A.G.
  3rd Echelon
    Base.

Enclosed I hand you
War Diaries for the periods
Feb & March. please

           [signature]
           Major OC

[stamp: 2/1ST NORTH MIDLAND FIELD COY. Date 7/4/17 R.E.]

Army Form C. 2118.

WAR DIARY
OF
INTELLIGENCE SUMMARY.
(Erase heading not required.)

Instructions regarding War Diaries and Intelligence
Summaries are contained in F.S. Regs., Part II.
and the Staff Manual respectively. Title pages
will be prepared in manuscript.

Vol II

March 1917

Hour, Date, Place	Summary of Events and Information	Remarks and references to Appendices
8.0.a.m. 1/3/17. BLANGY-TROUVILLE	Unit marched from BLANGY-TROUVILLE to WARFUSE-ABANCOURT and was quartered in huts.	
9.0.a.m. 2/3/17. WARFUSEE-ABANCOURT	O.C. and 2 S.O.R. left for FOUCAUCOURT to arrange for taking over from 7th field Co. R.E.	
11.0.a.m. 4/3/17. "	Inspection by Brigadier General Schieber C.E. 3rd Corps	
8.0.a.m. 6/3/17. "	1 Officer 13.O.R. No 3 Section left for VAIRE-SOUS-CORBIE for works at Divisional School	
9.0.a.m. 8/3/17. "	Remainder of No 3 Section proceeded to VAIRE-SOUS-CORBIE and attached to H.Q. 72 Army Field Artillery Bde.	
8.30.a.m. 9/3/17. "	Rest of Unit proceeded to FOUCAUCOURT and was quartered at CIMETIERE Camp.	
8.0.a.m. 10/3/17. FOUCAUCOURT to 18/3/17. "	Unit engaged in reserve area on hutting, roads and water supply.	
8.0.a.m. 19/3/17. ST. CHRIST.	Following German retirement Sections 1 & 4 proceeded to ST. CHRIST, made footbridge and commenced road Bridge across SOMME river and Canal at ST. CHRIST	
8.0.a.m. 20/3/17. FOUCAUCOURT	Section 3. returned from VAIRE-SOUS-CORBIE to FOUCAUCOURT	
9.0.a.m. 21/3/17. "	Unit proceeded to ST. CHRIST.	
8.0.a.m. 22/3/17. ST. CHRIST	Bridge for Infantry and 1st Line Transport made across SOMME river and Canal. Transport passed over 1.0 p.m. 22/3/17	
8.0.a.m. 22/3/17 to 27/3/17.	Heavy timber trestle bridge made across SOMME Canal at ST. CHRIST.	

Army Form C. 2118.

WAR DIARY
or
INTELLIGENCE SUMMARY.
(Erase heading not required.)

470 Field C.R.E.

March 1917

Hour, Date, Place		Summary of Events and Information	Remarks and references to Appendices
8.0 a.m. 22/3/17	ST. CHRIST.	Unit engaged on improving bridges and approaches and in arch repairs. VILLIERS – CARBONNEL – HAPPINCOURT – BRIOST – ST. CHRIST – TROY – ENNERMAIN – ATHIES.	
8.0 a.m. 23/3/17	"	Bridge constructed across OMIGNON river at ST CHRIST.	
8.0 a.m. 25/3/17	"	Service trestle bridge placed across OMIGNON river at ATHIES. Passage made round crater at ENNERMAIN	
8.0 a.m. 27/3/17 – 31/3/17		Heavy timber trestle bridge made at ATHIES to replace service trestle bridge.	

F. Fisher

A. Dicken
Major & O.C.

Instructions regarding War Diaries and Intelligence Summaries are contained in F.S. Regs., Part II. and the Staff Manual respectively. Title pages will be prepared in manuscript.

ORIGINAL
470 3rd Army R.E. 59
SM 3

Army Form C. 2118.

WAR DIARY
or
INTELLIGENCE SUMMARY.
(Erase heading not required.)

Instructions regarding War Diaries and Intelligence Summaries are contained in F.S. Regs., Part II. and the Staff Manual respectively. Title pages will be prepared in manuscript.

Place	Date	Hour	Summary of Events and Information	Remarks and references to Appendices
ST. CHRIST	1/4/17		No. 2 & 4 Section proceeded to ETERPIGNY from SOMME to take over from 469 Field C.R.E.	
"	2/4/17		Remainder of Unit proceeded to ETERPIGNY	
ETERPIGNY	3/4/17 to 5/4/17		Proceeded with construction of bridge over river SOMME & Canal at LAMIRE Farm	
ETERPIGNY	6/4/17		Unit proceeded to BOUVINCOURT. Commenced road diversions at craters at CATELET & BEAUMETZ	
BOUVINCOURT	7/4/17 to 13/4/17		Unit repairing and draining roads and filling in craters in areas CATELET, BEAUMETZ, BOUVINCOURT — HANCOURT — BERNES — VRAIGNES	
"	14/4/17		1.O. 32.O.R. of No. 3. Section proceeded to MONTIGNY for work with 176. Infantry Brigade, employed on deep dug-outs for Brigade H.Q.	
"	15/4/17 to 17/4/17		Sections 1, 2 & 4, repairing and draining roads and filling in craters	
"	18/4/17			
BOUVINCOURT	19/4/17	2.30 pm	1.O. & 33.O.R. of No.4 Section proceeded each to JEANCOURT for work with 176. Brigade, employed in making shelters for battalion H.Q. and in wiring main line	
"	"	6.0 pm	1.O. 26.O.R. No.1 Section proceeded to FOUCAUCOURT to take down and erect house huts.	
"	19/4/17 to 21/4/17		No. 2 Section employed on road repairs.	
"	22/4/17	4.0 pm	1.O. 26.O.R. of No.1 Section returned from FOUCAUCOURT on completion of work.	
"	23/4/17 to 26/4/17		Sections 1 & 2 employed on road repairs and erecting Aircraft huts at HANCOURT	
"	27/4/17	8.0 am	3. O.R. proceeded to FOUCAUCOURT and attached to III Corps School as instructors.	

Winter
Major. O.C

Original
Army Form C. 2118.

May 1917. 470 (2 Lr.) Field Co. R.E, T,

WAR DIARY
or
INTELLIGENCE SUMMARY.
(Erase heading not required.)

Instructions regarding War Diaries and Intelligence Summaries are contained in F.S. Regs., Part II. and the Staff Manual respectively. Title pages will be prepared in manuscript.

Hour, Date, Place	Summary of Events and Information	Remarks and references to Appendices
1 May to 6th. BOUVINCOURT	No. 1 & 2 Sections filling in Craters & erecting hursas at NOBESCOURT – BEAUMETZ – HANCOURT	
7 May "	The 2 Section proceeded to JEANCOURT to relieve No 4 Section Wiring	
8 to 24th "	The 4 Section returned from JEANCOURT to BOUVINCOURT Remainder of Unit engaged in repairing & metalling roads at HANCOURT – BEAUMETZ – NOBESCOURT to existing huts lat HANCOURT and BOUVINCOURT	
25th May "	3. O. and 11. OR proceeded to METZ-en-COUTURE to take over from the 4 28th. Field Co. R.E. Remainder of Unit road repairs & metalling roads at HANCOURT – BEAUMETZ	
26 – 27 May BOUVINCOURT	Remainder of Coy engaged in road repairs and metalling roads in Same cartel. 3. O.R. admitted to C.C.S.	
28 May "	Return of No 2 Section from JEANCOURT to BOUVINCOURT on completion of wiring work. Return of No 3 Section from MONTIGNY to JEANCOURT. Changed over for Cavalry Bdgr. H.Q. at JEANCOURT	
29. May. BOUVINCOURT	Unit proceeded to METZ-en-COUTURE	
30 – 31 METZ en COUTURE	Company engaged at works on C.T.O. in rear of BILHEM Farm.	

J. Parker
Major. O.C

Original

WAR DIARY
or
INTELLIGENCE SUMMARY

Army Form C. 2118.

470 (N.MID) Field Coy R.E.

for June 1917

(Erase heading not required.)

Instructions regarding War Diaries and Intelligence Summaries are contained in F.S. Regs., Part II. and the Staff Manual respectively. Title Pages will be prepared in manuscript.

Place	Date	Hour		Summary of Events and Information	Remarks and references to Appendices
		FROM	TO		
METZ en COUTURE	June 1.	June 1	11	Ref. Map Sheet 57C S.E. Sections 1. & 4 attached to 178 Infantry Brigade for work on front line system in Left Brigade Sector from BILHEM Farm to BEAUCAMP. Q.5C.37 to Q.12.b.0.4. Captain C.J.B. DAVIS appointed to act as liaison officer with 178th Brigade. Section 3 engaged on baths at METZ en COUTURE and erecting elephant shelters in Brigade H.Q. in HAVRINCOURT Wood Q.15.C.	
METZ en COUTURE	11	11	12	178th Infantry Brigade relieved by 176 Brigade. Sections 1 & 4 attached to 176 Brigade. Reinforcements join Unit.	
"	12	12	30	Section 2. Continued work on O.Ts in rear. Section 3. Continued work on Bgde N.Q.	
"	26	-		Section 3. Completed Brigade N.Q.	29/6/17. 2 men killed by shell fire.
"	27	27	30	No 3 platoon of 175 Labour Company attached to Unit for repair of METZ-en-COUTURE – TRESCAULT Road.	
"	27	27	30	Section 3 clearing old pumping plant from well at beer factory at METZ-en-COUTURE Q.25.b.58 and preparing for installation of new pump.	

Fisher
Major. O.C

ORIGINAL

Army Form C. 2118.

WAR DIARY
or
INTELLIGENCE SUMMARY.
(Erase heading not required.)

470 Field Coy. R.E.

July 1917

Instructions regarding War Diaries and Intelligence Summaries are contained in F.S. Regs., Part II. and the Staff Manual respectively. Title pages will be prepared in manuscript.

Hour, Date, Place	Summary of Events and Information	Remarks and references to Appendices
July 1-8 METZ-EN-COUTURE	Nos. 1 & 4 Sections improving & draining C.T.s in rear	Map Ref. Sheet 57 c S.E.
" 1-8 do.	No. 3 Section installing pump at Beet Factory Q.25 b.5.8.	
" 1-6 do.	No. 2 " repairing METZ-EN-COUTURE – TRESCAULT road	
July 6	No. 2 " proceeded to LE MESNIL-EN-ARROUAISE to assist in preparation of Brigade Camp.	
" 6	1 Off. & 4 O.R. of 511th Field Coy. R.E. take over from this unit.	
July 9 LE MESNIL-EN- ARROUAISE	Unit proceeds to LE MESNIL-EN-ARROUAISE & encamps for rest & training. Camp at O.35 d. Sheet 57c S.W.	
July 16 "	Six reinforcements join Unit.	
" 10-25 "	General improvements in camp area – building in- cinerators & latrines, repairing roads etc., Training programme carried out. Includes set- ting consolidation of positions, bayonet exercises, musketry & general recreation	
July 24th "	M.C.Os co-operate with 178th Inf. Brig. in Tactical Ex.	
" 25 "	Quick wiring demonstration	
" 27 & 30 "	Unit co-operates with 178 Brig. in Tactical Exercise	
" 31 "	No. 1 – consolidation of positions &c. Training programme continued	

V. C. Ledger
Capt. for
Major & O.C.

ORIGINAL

Army Form C. 2118.

WAR DIARY
or
INTELLIGENCE SUMMARY.
(Erase heading not required.)

August 1914

470TH FIELD COY R.E.

Place	Date Aug	Hour	Summary of Events and Information	Remarks and references to Appendices
LE MESNIL- EN- ARROUAISE	1st to 15th		General Training Programme carried out consisting of Bayonet exercises, Consolidating & Wiring.	Vol 7
"	2nd 6th		Officers & NCOs engaged in 198th Brigade Tactical Exercise, No 2 Section on Brigade Baths. Company engaged in 59th Divisional Tactical Exercise No 2 consisting of Consolidating trenching and Wiring.	
"	8th		Company inspected by C.R.E. 59th Div.	
"	11th		Sections 1 and 4 engaged on 198th Brigade Tactical Scheme.	
"	13th & 14th		Erection of Huts & Baths for 194th Brigade by Sections 3rd & D	
"	15th		General Inspection of three field boys by G.O.C. near BARASTRE 01.Y.B6585 Ref Map Sheet 57k S.W. 1/20,000	
LE TRANSLOY	15th to 22nd		Company proceeds to LE TRANSLOY. In hutted camp at N18C62. Ref Map 57C S W 1/20,000 Company engaged in the construction of Rifle Range at LE TRANSLOY Work on Rifle Range handed over to 2nd Siege Coy Royal Anglesea R.E.	
	23rd		2.O.R. Advance party to BOUZINCOURT.	
BOUZINCOURT	24th to 30th		Company proceeds to BOUZINCOURT. Quartered in hutted camp at G.H. 6.3 Ref Map Lens 11 1/10,000	
	28th		General Training programme carried out consisting of Gas Drill, Route Marches & Physical Drill &c. 1.O. and 2.O.R. Advance Party to WINNEZEELE	

Frazier
Major & OC
470th Field Coy R.E.

Original

Army Form C. 2118.

WAR DIARY
or
INTELLIGENCE SUMMARY.

(Erase heading not required.)

470th FIELD COY R.E.

Vol VIII SEPT 1917

Instructions regarding War Diaries and Intelligence Summaries are contained in F. S. Regs., Part II. and the Staff Manual respectively. Title pages will be prepared in manuscript.

Place	Date	Hour	Summary of Events and Information	Remarks and references to Appendices
BOUZINCOURT	1st Sept	1.30	Unit moves to and entrains at BEAUCOURT thence by rail to GODEWAERSVELDE. Detrained at GODEWAERSVELDE and moved to OUDEZEELE at J.1.d.9.v. N of CASSEL	
OUDE ZEELE	2nd to 10th		General Training carried out	
WINNEZEELE	11th to 19th		Nos 1 & 3 Sections with No Divisional Baths at WINNEZEELE. Completion of Baths	
WATOU	20th & 22nd		Unit moves to WATOU No 2 Area. L.f. B.H.	
YPRES	24th		Unit moves to YPRES and take over from 423rd Field Coy All Sections engaged on strengthening Mule tracks No 6 at WIELTJE FARM	REF. MAP FREZENBERG ED 3
	25th		Nos 1 & 4 Sections engaged on repairing No 6 Mule track and extending it to CORN HILL C.18.D.29 No.2 & 3 -do- -do- C.29 a & C.23d No 5 -do- -do- Duck-boarding Party of 1 O. 60 O.R. Seaforth Pioneers attached, engaged on repairs to the 6 Mule track and extending same to POND FARM GALLERY C.18.B.91	
	26th		Unit engaged in action at ZONNEBEKE & GRAFENSTAFEL RIDGE in conjunction with 148th Brigade 59th Division. All Objectives gained viz LEVI COTTAGES, VAN ISACKER FARM DOCHY-OTTO-TORONTO and RIVERSIDE FARMS. 4 Sections (in attack) attached to 6, 8, 5 Battalions Yorks. Derbys 148 Bde engaged on consolidating strong-points at C.14. C.4.H Casualties O/c and 1 O.R. Killed 18 O.R. wounded	
	27th 28th 29th		Unit engaged on repairing Mule-track No 6 to SCHULER GALLERY and track made to KANSAS HOUSE Deviation to CLIFTON HOUSE taken out and track made over the HANNEBEKE RIVER. Dug-outs of Bde H.Q. at CAPRICORN KEEP improved and Sandbagged. Repairing and widening Mule Track from SCHULER GALLERY to KANSAS House and Duck boarding same. Sandbagging & strengthening CAPRICORN KEEP. Attached Seaford Pioneer (9th) engaged on widening track from SCHULER GALLERIES to OLIVE HOUSE and strengthening track to HANNEBEKE. Geo from & family completing at CAPRICORN KEEP	
	30th		Unit relieved by N.Z. Div. R.E. and proceeds to HOP. FACTORY AT H.E. a.5.9.	

N Kinnagan Capt RE OC

Original

Army Form C. 2118.

WAR DIARY
or
INTELLIGENCE SUMMARY.

(Erase heading not required.)

470 (1/1) FIELD COY. R.E.

Instructions regarding War Diaries and Intelligence Summaries are contained in F.S. Regs., Part II and the Staff Manual respectively. Title pages will be prepared in manuscript.

Place	Date	Hour	Summary of Events and Information	Remarks and references to Appendices
VLAMATINGHE SEATON CAMP	Oct 1st		Unit moves to WATOU M92 Area SEATON CAMP F.5.b. Sheet 27.	A.R.
"	2nd		I.O. (Reinforcement) joined Unit	A.R.
"	3rd		Unit moves to BOESEGHEM 4.F.15.a.a. Ref. HAZEBROUCH 5.A.	A.R.
LA LOVIE	4th		" " " DELETTE C.55.d.4.5 " HAZEBROUCH 5.A.	A.R.
BOESEGHEM	5th		" " " BAILLEUL-AUMERVAL E.6.b.b. " "	A.R.
DELETTE	5th & 10th		" " " HESTRUS	A.R.
BAILLEUL	11th		[Advance party proceed to CARENCY and take over from 1st Canadian Field Coy 4th Canadian Div Engineers.	A.R.
HESTRUS	12 & 13		BARLIN	A.R.
BARLIN	14th		CARENCY X.18.a.27 No 1+2 Sections engaged on making Dug outs	A.R.
CARENCY	15th-16th		and Duck-boarding trenches at S.6.d.40.90 No 3 & 4 Section making new Trade from SOUCHEZ-GIVENCHY Rd 36c SW. S.4.d.65.95 also at S.8.C.4.8 in conjunction with 144th Infantry Brigade.	A.R.
	18th to 23rd		(Reinforcements) Major C.B. Laikes commenced Making transept and laying trench - towards from GIVENCHY RD to RED TRENCH S.12.d.95 Constructing Tullery on CLUCAS TRENCH and RED TRENCH S.10.A.2.4	C.R.
			Cleaning CLUCAS Trench and Approach Same between L.T RAILWAY and GIVENCHY RD MAP REF S.10 Leading and unloading trucks of slag at FOSSE 6. and FOSSE CROSS. Making Cart road.	C.R.
CARENCY	24th to 26th		Revetting, Duck-boarding deepening CLUCAS TRENCH from Commencement to GIVENCHY in conjunction with 144th Brigade. Loading slag Dr.A & breaking same on New road Attendance SOUCHEZ and GIVENCHY over VIMY RIDGE S.8.d.0.5	C.R.
			M.S. Emplacement commenced at CRAZY REDOUBT M.29.K.9.5	C.R.
			Improved entrance SOUCHEZ road M.28.C.14	C.R.
	27 & 28 & 29		M.G. Emplacement completed at M.29.K.9.5 Continuation of work begun the 15th in conjunction with 144th Brigade	C.R.

A5534 Wt. W4473 M687. 750,000 8/16 D.D. & L. Ltd. Forms/C.2118/13.

Army Form C. 2118.

WAR DIARY
or
INTELLIGENCE SUMMARY.
(Erase heading not required.)

Original

470TH (N.M.) FIELD COY. R.E.   Vol 10

Place	Date	Hour	Summary of Events and Information	Remarks and references to Appendices
CARENCY	Nov 1st to		Employed on Digging, draining, revetting, duck-boarding & Berming LUCAS TRENCH S.5.a.5.4. and RED TRENCH S.5.a.23.55. Map 36c. S.W.	J.R.
"	Nov 6th		Constructing & completing fire-bays and relaying duck-boards RED TRENCH S.5.d.8.5. Employed on flue-bed, shredding slag, making rent and laying boards road between SOUCHEZ and GIVENCHY.	J.R.
"	6th-9th		Draining, clearing and duck-boarding CRAZY REDOUBT and BEAUMONT REDOUBT M.23.b.8.4. and M.30.a.8.8.	J.R.
"	9th to 10th		Digging battle trench, laying cable & filling in at M.35.a. CITÉ ABATTOIR. Wiring commenced at M.35.b.4.7. to M.29.a.9.5, S.L.b.1.8. to M.36.d.5.4.5, M.35.b.25. to M.29.a.1.44.	J.R.
"	11th to 13th		General continuation of previous work commenced.	J.R.
"	14th-18th		Employed on Digging, draining, revetting, duck-boarding & Berming CADGER TRENCH M.36.a.50.25. also DAWSON trench M.36.a.2.9.	J.R.
"			Clearing & duck-boarding CRONY REDOUBT M.23.b.8.4.	J.R.
"			Duck-boarding & cleaning out CRONY CROOK M.17.d.4.0.	J.R.
"			Handing over the above work to 1st CANADIAN FIELD COY. R.E.	J.R.
GOUY-EN-ARTOIS	19th		Unit proceeds to GOUY-EN-ARTOIS	J.R.
BLARVILLE	20. 22nd		Unit proceeds to BLARVILLE X.4.a.8.5. and GOMIECOURT B.10.a.45.05. (Tactical Train)	J.R.
EQUANCOURT	23rd 24th		— do — to EQUANCOURT	J.R.
GOUZEACOURT	25th to 29th		— do — to GOUZEACOURT Q.30.c.7.2. and with one company of 178th Brigade engaged in constructing & erecting huts at FISH CAMP, making & repairing road to same. Unit reformed	J.R.
EQUANCOURT	30th		Unit proceeds to FLESQUIERES K.18.6.5.6	J.R.

L. Bohman
Major O.C.

Army Form C. 2118.

Original

WAR DIARY or INTELLIGENCE SUMMARY.

(Erase heading not required.)

479th (North Midland) Field Coy. R.E.

DECEMBER 1917

Place	Date	Hour	Summary of Events and Information	Remarks and references to Appendices
EQANCOURT	30.11.17 to Dec 2/17	10 A.M.	Unit proceeds to FLESQUIERES via GOUZEAUCOURT (Map ref G3b) of which the enemy had taken possession. O.C. Coy was ordered by G.O.C. 29th Div to at once advance & hold our air positions under reinforcements arrived when there was a general advance made on the enemy who however ran out of GOUZEAUCOURT beyond the village of GONNELIEU. Casualties of Coy. 1 O. Prisoner of War. 11. O.R. wounded. 1.O.R. missing. 6.O.R. killed.	JR
YTRES.	Dec 3/17 to Dec 6/17.		Unit moves to YTRES & then proceeds to TRESCAULT (Q.10.A.52). Engaged in making shelters & dug outs, making up & wiring support trenches across the HINDENBURG Support Line. No 1 Section engaged in demolishing enemy guns at (FLESQUIERES)	JR
TRESCAULT	Dec 7/17 to Dec 9/17		Casualties 1.O.R. killed 2 O.R. wounded. Casualties 1.O.R. killed 1 O.R. wounded.	JR JR
FLESQUIERES	Dec 10/17 to Dec 28/17		Unit takes over HINDENBURG front line work from 467 & 469 Field Companies (59 Div) engaged in conjunction with 177th & 178th Bgdes (working parties) widening & deepening trenches, draining & wiring 3 Batts. I Section engaged on S.O.P. C.T. completed. Area of above work K.17.D. to K. L.13? Casualties 1 O.R. killed. 1.O.R. wounded. O.C. hands over work to the 93rd Field Coy R.E. Div.	JR JR JR
BEAULINCOURT	Dec 28/17 Dec 29/17		Unit moves to BEAULINCOURT. Unit entrains at BAPAUME & proceeds to TINQUES area & billeted at MONCHEAUX. transport at RUNEVILLE.	JR JR
MONCHEAUX	Dec 30/17 to Dec 31/17.		Unit engaged on Physical training, General training, instructing 176 Bgde in wiring, trenching & bivouacking.	JR

Signature
Major, O.C.

Date 30.12.17
479th (NORTH MIDLAND) FIELD COY.

Original

Army Form C. 2118.

WAR DIARY
or
INTELLIGENCE SUMMARY. 470. FIELD.Co.R.E

JANUARY/1918.

(Erase heading not required.)

Instructions regarding War Diaries and Intelligence Summaries are contained in F. S. Regs., Part II. and the Staff Manual respectively. Title pages will be prepared in manuscript.

Place	Date	Hour	Summary of Events and Information	Remarks and references to Appendices
MONCHEAUX	Jan 1st to Jan 12		Unit engaged on Physical Training, Bayonet fighting & General Training. Instruction given to 178 Brigade in Wiring, Trenching & Consolidating. Repairing billets in villages within 178 Brigade Area	Green
	Jan 13 to Jan 25		Instruction given to 178 Brigade in Wiring etc. Unit engaged in Physical, Section & Company Drill. Series of Lectures by Officers & Senior N.C.O.s given to all ranks. Subjects' Discipline, Wiring, Map-reading etc. Repairs continued in villages within 178 Brigade Area.	Green
	Jan 26 to Jan 31		Unit engaged in Physical, Section & Company Drill. Instruction given to 178 Brigade in Wiring etc. Repairs completed in villages within 178 Brigade Area. Instruction given to Unit in working of Lewis Gun, Demolitions, Laying out of Trenches & Wiring.	Green

G.F.R.Wilks 1st for MAJOR R.E.
OC 470 Fld.Cy R.E.

Army Form C. 2118.

WAR DIARY
or
INTELLIGENCE SUMMARY.

(Erase heading not required.)

410TH FIELD. COY. R.E. T.

FEBRUARY 1918

Vol 13

Original

Place	Date	Hour	Summary of Events and Information	Remarks and references to Appendices
MONCHEAUX	1-6		General Machine Gun Instruction (175 M.G. Co. 178 Bgde)	
"	4. & 8		Advance party proceeds to ST.LEGER 28.C.9.1. to take over from 229 FIELD.Co.RE. 40.D.	
BARLY	9-12		Unit proceeds to BARLY P.5.a.55 Billet.	
MERCATEL	12.		" " MERCATEL M.23.C.25 Billet.	
ST LEGER	12-16		" " ST.LEGER. Nos. 2, 3, 4, Section take over relief at CHALK Pit U.19.a.2.3.	
"	"		No.1.Section with H.Qrs billet at T.28.C.9.1. No.2 Section engaged on Right Batt" Sub Sect" (in Conjunction with 178. Inf. Bgde) Clearing, Widening, and deepening JENFIN, PIONEER, BORDERER & GOLLYWOG Trenches.	
"	16-19		Nos 3 4 Section. Wiring & digging ECOUST SWITCH Double Apron completed	
"	"		Continuation of work completed. I/M Emplacements. STRAY SUPPORT. Wiring FRONT Line. and Anteboarding and chaining same. Benning BURG SUPPORT, JOVE, BOW, Bane POST made, and TIGER Trench joined to junction PELICAN AVENUE (V.20.C.95)(V.20b)(V.14.8)	
"	19-21		Wiring closed apron fence in TIGER (V.26.b.29) PELICAN.AVE (V.26.b.3.2) STRAY SUPPORT. V.20.a.4.4 Digging, Benning & Chaining KNUCKLE AVENUE. V.14.d.10.25. and connecting BURG SUPPORT to FRONT LINE (V.14.d.)	
"	"		Making Maud Stations and mattress Benning VALLEY SUP. V.20.d.6978. Beginning, Benning MARS LANE (V.B.28.) and Continuation of Work on enclosure Brickworks Begining Fire Trench TIGER TRCH — MAN SUPPORT Salvaging material for STRAY SUPPORT.(V.13.a.) Wiring etc. No.1 Section relieve No 2. at V.19.a.2.3	
"	22-23		General improvements at H.Qrs Bullet. Enlargement of Bath at T.28.C.9.1. under new plan.	
"	"		Continuation of Works in progress. Benning, deepening sloping VALLEY SUPPORT. V.20.d.76 Improvements to Gas Chambers for R.F.A. making IN.GrO for Sm. Co. V.75. V.25 a.47.	
"	24 to 26		General progress on Works in hand. Receiving and Benning VALLEY Trench V.20.d.58 making T.M.G emplacements V.21.C.32. Completing O.P at V.14.C Central, and mattress etc. V.25.a. 60.65. Improving, digging & widening TIGER Trench. 26.b.2.8 - 29.C.10.00.	
"	27-28			

W Wright
Major O.C.

59th Divisional Engineers

WAR DIARY

470th (N.M.) FIELD COMPANY R.E.

MARCH 1 9 1 8

WAR DIARY or INTELLIGENCE SUMMARY

Army Form C. 2118.
ORIGINAL

MARCH 1918

470th N.M. FIELD Co R.E. (T.)

Place	Date	Hour	Summary of Events and Information	Remarks and references to Appendices
ST LEGER	1		Standing our front line U20D to 208th FIELD Co RE 34th DIVISION.	
	2		Unit marched to MORY 82.b.43	
	3	610	Erection of camp & Brigade HQ in area. Inter-change of NOREUIL SWITCH line with 176th, 177th & 178th BRIGADES, C5e 7.8 - C15 a 9.7. Living dug-outs in BATTLE ZONE, making Emergency Roads, 2nd & 13th systems. Laying ANTI-TANK MINEFIELD at C5 c 5-7. Hundred 600 in length laid by 7th HUSSARS Section. No 1, 2 & 4 taken over RIGHT-SUB-SECTOR from 467th FIELD Co RE C16 c F.2	
NOREUIL	116			
	20th		Unit engaged in strengthening defences in 12th & 2nd systems, PARKGRANT NEWSBURY, HOBART, NOREUIL SWITCH, HORSE SHOE TRENCH, MACHINE GUN emplacements at RAILWAY RESERVE and A.D.S. at NOREUIL.	
NOREUIL	21		Enemy attacked. Company manned Emergency Post, NOREUIL but were outnumbered. F.O.C. Company), Lt. WINGS & three men returned to REAR HQ MORY. Remainder missing and Lt. L.W. HULSE, 2/Lt & O/S Kemp and J.W. ENGLISH, C.S.M., A.B. SWALLOW.	
AYETTE	21		TRANSPORT moved to AYETTE. No 3 Sect Mining at ERVILLERS 6 dug line.	
	22		No 3 Sect in field at AYETTE.	
	23		Company retired to BOUZINCOURT by march route	
BOUZINCOURT	25		Company moved to PONT NOYELLES by march route	
PONT NOYELLES	27		" " " MONTRELET "	
MONTRELET	26		" " " CANDAS & HERMIN by M? transport	
HERMIN	30			
	31		Inspection by H.M. the KING at HERMIN. Until army congratulated on its work by H.M. 12th Stage 6 LILLERS & 2nd Army Area.	

59th Divisional Engineers

470th FIELD COMPANY R. E.

APRIL 1918.

ORIGINAL

Army Form C. 2118.

WAR DIARY
or
INTELLIGENCE SUMMARY.
(Erase heading not required.)

APRIL 1918
470 FIELD CO. R.E.

WR/5

Place	Date	Hour	Summary of Events and Information	Remarks and references to Appendices
HERMAN	1.		Unit entrained at AUBIGNY, detrained at PROVEN	AR
WATOU	2-3		" proceed to WATOU N° 2 Area. Reinforcements 3.o.r.	AR
	4-7		Company entrained at ST QUENTIN and proceed to ST JEAN YPRES. H.Q at I.2.b.4.5. Transport	AR
ST JEAN YPRES	8		lines at I.1.a.2.4. Unit relieves 222nd Field Co. R.E. and take over posts from 510 LONDON. FIELD CO RE	AR
"	10		at D.17.c.4.3. – D.18.a.7.8. – D.18.a.15.15. Engaged on sandbagging, revetting, making XPM gabions (Sheet 27) AR	AR
"	12		repairing duckboards and pumps (army huts) at above defences. Reinforcements 58.o.r.	AR
			Reinforcements 26.o.r. Casualties 2 o.r. Wounded.	AR
LOCRE	12		Unit proceeds to LOCRE	AR
	13		" " KEMMEL. Engaged on making POSTS in FRONT & RESERVE lines	AR
KEMMEL	14		in conjunction with 173 Brigade attached the 19 Div. KEMMEL HILL defences	AR
"	15–		Made and manned RESERVE Trench at N.25.C.23 (Sheet 28) Casualties 3.o.r. Killed	AR
"	18		11. o.r. Wounded.	AR
"	19		Unit relieved by French Div. and proceeds to WESTOUTRE – ELVERDINGE – HOUTKERQUE	AR
HOUTKERQUE	21–		H.Q.Qr.M at D.24.b.99. Coy engaged in Physical & General Training	AR
"	to		Unit engaged in making posts in ARMY line in WATOU Area	AR
	6.27		Coy. Quarters in ST JANS-TER-BIEZEN	AR
ST JANS-TER-BIEZEN	28		Unit engaged in making NEW line RENINGHELST – BOESCHEPE	AR
	to			
	30.			

J Cohman
Major O.C. 470 F.C.
27 May 1918

ORIGINAL

Army Form C. 2118.

WAR DIARY
or
INTELLIGENCE SUMMARY.
(Erase heading not required.)

MAY 1918
470th N.M. FIELD Cy R.E. (T)

Vol 16

Instructions regarding War Diaries and Intelligence Summaries are contained in F. S. Regs., Part II. and the Staff Manual respectively. Title pages will be prepared in manuscript.

Place	Date May	Hour	Summary of Events and Information	Remarks and references to Appendices
ST JANTER BIEZEN	1-5		Coy engaged on digging Anny Line at L 35 Sh.27. Continuation of work at L 33 with 177th Inf. Bde.	AR AR AR AR
HOUTKERQUE	6		Unit moved to HOUTKERQUE.	AR
ST OMER	7.8		Unit moved to ST OMER. H.Q. at Cavalry Barracks. (awaiting Army Instructions)	AR
REBECQ	9		Unit moved to REBECQ	AR
BOURS	10		Unit moved to BOURS	AR
DIEVAL	11		Unit moved to DIEVAL	AR
MAGNIL LE RUITE	12 6-31"		Unit moved to Camp in Bois de Obras Sq A59 Sh 36 3. Company engaged on S.H.Q. dugouts (B.B LINE) (No 2 Subsector). Extension of Cheriso Intercom in preparation, wiring trenches, throwing tracks & M.G. emplacements. Somewhat cleared through woods & construction of dead ken. Low wiring somewhere wire put out in front of firing line.	AR AR

(signature)
(Major RE(T))
O.C. 470th (N.M.) FIELD Cy R.E.

ORIGINAL

Army Form C. 2118.

WAR DIARY or INTELLIGENCE SUMMARY.
(Erase heading not required.)

JUNE 1918   470TH FIELD CO R.E. T.

Hour, Date, Place	Summary of Events and Information	Remarks and references to Appendices
BOIS-de-OLHAIN 1-29 to	Unit engaged on A. Sector B.B Line, in making trenches, strong points and wiring of same	LR
BOIS-de-OLHAIN 30.	2.0. 5q.O.R. Sections 1 & 3 proceed to CREPY, and report to 59(Divl) School for instructional duties	LR

L Rahming
Major. O.C.

ORIGINAL

Army Form C. 2118.

WAR DIARY
or
INTELLIGENCE SUMMARY.
(Erase heading not required.)

JULY 1918

470TH FIELD COY R.E.

WO 1/8

Place	Date	Hour	Summary of Events and Information	Remarks and references to Appendices
BOIS D' OLHAIN	1-10		Unit engaged in construction of B.B. line. Afterwards a Secret AP	AR
CABERS PREDEFIN CREPY	19th 24th		Nos 1 & 3 Sections moved to CREPY, 7 engaged in entrenching important "B" of 9th DIVISION – field works.	AR
			"B" of 9th DIVISION – field works.	AR
HOUDAIN	10th		Remainder of Unit moved to HOUDAIN to take over work of 2nd FIELD Squadron on B Sector B.B. LINE.	AR
"	15th		Shortie aerocraft bombed camp. Casualties Khomas 28.	AR
PREDEFIN	28th		Unit moved to PREDEFIN where Nos 1 & 3 Section rejoined the company.	AR
BELLACOURT	24		Unit moved to BELLACOURT. Took over billets of 81st BATTN C.E. with H.Qrs at CHATEAU R51.c 85.90.	AR
	25		Nos 1, 2, 3, 4 & 5 in take over forward billets reconnaissance work on Strong Points & Dugouts in DIVISIONAL AREA from 81st BATTN C.E.	AR
	26		No. 3 Section taken over new work from 9th BATTN C.E., reconnoitre demolitions.	AR
	30		Nos 1 & 4 Sections commence work on C.T. Bordeaux Avenue.	AR
	31		18 O.R. reinforcements	AR

H. Chapman
MAJOR R.E.(T)
Or. O. 470TH FIELD Co. R. E.

WAR DIARY

47th North Midland Field Coy R.E.

INTELLIGENCE SUMMARY. 470 FIELD CO. R.E.

AUGUST. 1918.

Hour, Date, Place	Summary of Events and Information	Remarks and references to Appendices
BELLACOURT Aug 1st to 20th	Continuation of work on dugouts strong points, communication & dumping magns in 53 R35 R34 R29 52 M27	A.R.
21st	Recce Mellou Trestle Bridge across Cojeul R. at Boisleux St Marc, dumbbelled & double elbow to Cemetery & Autheary. Enemy gas shelled forward. Bridge completed between 9pm & 4am. SH 51c 675.65	W.C. 51B. S.W. A.R.
22nd	Carrying gaps in wire shielding Infantry Bridges across front line trench. Jumping-off trench marked out for Infantry. 300x of front opened.	Sheet 51B. S.W. A.R.
23rd	Unit travelled to SAULTY to entrain. Returned to open	A.R.
24th	Entrained SAULTY, detrained BERGUETTE for MARQUEVILLE	A.R.
25th 26th	MARQUEVILLE	A.R.
27th ROBECQ	Unit marches by road march to ROBECQ near HQ at P23.04.1. forward Billets CALONNE SUR LA LYS G14 87.5. Took over from 439th FIELD G.R.E.	Sheet 36 & A.R.
28th	Engaged in bridging operation of Bdes & Battalion HQ	A.R.
29th	roads, maintenance & clearing ruins, ROBECQ &	A.R.
30th 31	CALONNE SUR LA LYS	A.R.
	15 CALONNE SUR LA LYS myself & Lieut Frost the R.E.W.E. officers in enemy trenches & mined	Lt. Col. Malmesbury
		470 Field CRE.

Army Form C. 2118.

WAR DIARY
or
INTELLIGENCE SUMMARY

(Erase heading not required.)

SEPTEMBER 1918
470TH FIELD COMPANY.

Instructions regarding War Diaries and Intelligence Summaries are contained in F. S. Regs., Part II. and the Staff Manual respectively. Title Pages will be prepared in manuscript.

Place	Date	Hour	Summary of Events and Information	Remarks and references to Appendices
CALONNE	1-3		Building bridges at S.110.7.8. Thiel 51.6 R15 D2.8 R18.25.6 R9011 R15 D34 R9B8.6 L34 B5.7 Feet 36A Retaining runds, fixing up windows in Divisional Area.	R
ESTREM	4		Unit moved to R.9.D.7.6 completed elsewhere.	R
	5-30		Taking over strip window frames, house cleanings Brigade HQ, Divisional HQ, & concrete dugouts for RAM.C. & Brigade HQ in Divisional Area.	R

2449 Wt. W14957/M90 750,000 1/16 J.B.C. & A. Forms/C.2118/12.

1st Div. C.R.E. Field Coy Signals

October 1918

Army Form C. 2118.

WAR DIARY
or
INTELLIGENCE SUMMARY 470TH FIELD. COY R.E.
(Erase heading not required.)

OCTOBER 1918

Place	Date	Hour	Summary of Events and Information	Remarks and references to Appendices
LEOTREN	1-2		Unit engaged on completion of accommodation for Infantry.	AR
	3		Unit moved to CUT DE SAC FARM G8C92 Sheet 36	AR
FLEURBAIX	4		" " " to FLEURBAIX Sheet 36. Engaged on	AR
	5-18		making roads tracks at WEZ MACQUART, fixing on various various tramroads	AR
			generally tracks for Brigading.	
MARQUETTE	18		Unit moved to MARQUETTE, should fabten & trestle Bridge at ST ANDRE	AR
	19		Unit moved to H&M. Bridge for 12tn apple loads constructed across R. MARQUE	AR
			at L' HEMPONPONT.	
TEMPLEUVE	20		Unit moved to TEMPLEUVE Sheet 37. Engaged on roads enclose &	AR
	21-24		restoring roads.	
TOUFFLERS	24		Unit moved to G24.c.4.9 are engaged on general training.	AR
	-30		No 2 Section moved to ST ANDRE last inonth bridge upstream bridge	AR
	25,29		on avenue with bridging equipment.	

Fleurbaix
Major R.E.
470 Fd Co d/c 1.11.18.

2449 Wt. W14957/M90 750,000 1/16 J.B.C. & A. Forms/C.2118/12.

WAR DIARY ORIGINAL or INTELLIGENCE SUMMARY.

Army Form C. 2118.

Date: NOVEMBER 1918

470th Field Coy R.E.

Vol 22

Hour, Date, Place		Summary of Events and Information	Remarks and references to Appendices
1-9	TOUFFLERS	Company engaged on training in Bridging and such. 178th Infantry Brigade on advance reconnaissance at RAMEGNIES-CHIN, ANVAING, MOURCOURT.	R.
9	OBIGIES	Company advanced with forward Brigade. Engaged firing in cradles removing booby traps & demolitions.	R.
-12	LEUZE	Unit moved by march route to LEUZE. Engaged in reconstruction of railway between LEUZE & LIGNE.	R.
12-18			R.
18	KAIN	Unit moved by march route to KAIN	R.
19	TEMPLEUVE	Unit moved by march route to TEMPLEUVE	R.
20	PETIT RONCHIN	Unit moved by march route to PETIT RONCHIN	R.
-30		Engaged on making furniture for Divisional Club and carrying out General training.	R.
28		No 4 Section moved to BRUAY to prepare huts for move of 178th Infantry Brigade.	R.

P Robinson
Major O.C.
470th Field Coy R.E.

470 Fd Coy R.E.

DECEMBER 1918. Army Form C. 2118.

WAR DIARY
or
INTELLIGENCE SUMMARY.

(Erase heading not required.)

Instructions regarding War Diaries and Intelligence Summaries are contained in F.S. Regs., Part II. and the Staff Manual respectively. Title pages will be prepared in manuscript.

Hour, Date, Place	Summary of Events and Information	Remarks and references to Appendices
1-3. PETIT ROCHIN.	Company engaged on recreational & renewal training	
3.	Company moved to Camp at VAUDRICOURT.	
4-31. VAUDRICOURT.	Engaged on repairs to to camps, water supply &c in Divisional Area.	
27. VAUDRICOURT.	Nos. 1-3.4 Sections moved to BOUVIGNY and were engaged in dismantling huts at BOUVIGNY, BOYEFFLES and HOULETTE WOOD.	
10. VAUDRICOURT.	2 Officers & 23 O.R. proceeded to MINX WORKSHOPS to form instructional staff for Div'l R.E. School.	

Sudb Salmon
Capt.
O.C. 470 Field Co R.E.

Army Form C. 2118.

WAR DIARY
or
INTELLIGENCE SUMMARY.

(Erase heading not required.) 470TH FIELD Co. R.E.

JAN. 1919

Instructions regarding War Diaries and Intelligence Summaries are contained in F.S. Regs., Part II. and the Staff Manual respectively. Title pages will be prepared in manuscript.

Hour, Date, Place		Summary of Events and Information	Remarks and references to Appendices
VAUDRICOURT	1 JAN	Unit engaged on dismantling huts in Bn Sit Camp.	
"	2	12 OR Reinforcements	
"	5	No 1, 2 & 3 Sections proceed to OLHAIN. Engaged on erection of Dambrigahni Horse Standings. Construction of same nearing upon comp.	
"	1-31	3 Officers & 111 OR sent to dispersal area for demob.	
"	24	12 OR engaged at 59 DIV R.E. School reform	
"		Unit.	
"	24-31	Unit engaged on dismantling & erection of huts in B.E. Area.	

F. W. Crosby Newport
Lieut. [signature]
MAJOR R.E. 411
470TH FIELD CO R.E.

To:
D A S 3rd Echelon.

War Diary

I herewith enclose
War Diary of this Unit
for the month of April/19

Capt R.E.

WAR DIARY
or
INTELLIGENCE SUMMARY.
(Erase heading not required.)

Army Form C. 2118.

FEBRUARY
470TH FIELD Co. R.E.

Hour, Date, Place	Summary of Events and Information	Remarks and references to Appendices
VAUDRICOURT 1 Feb.	Unit entrain at NOEUX LES MINES and proceed to ETAPLES	
ETAPLES 1-28.	Engaged in R.E. workshops and Works Service L. of C.	

H. F. Green
O.C. 470th Field Coy R.E.

To G.O.C.
British Troops F. & F.
War Diary.

I herewith attach the
above for this Unit
please

A.H. Miller, Lt. OC.

ORIGINAL

WAR DIARY
or
INTELLIGENCE SUMMARY

(Erase heading not required.)

Army Form C. 2118.

470 FIELD COY
APRIL 1919

JUL 27 59

Place	Date	Hour	Summary of Events and Information	Remarks and references to Appendices
ETAPLES	1st to 23rd		Unit engaged on R.E. Workshops and Yard and Work Service L.B.C.	C.W.M.
	6th		Two officers proceed to C.E. 3rd Clearing up Area	W.M.M.
	9th		Two officers proceed to PERONNE & CAMBRAI SUB-AREAS	W.M.M.
	23rd		Unit entrain at ETAPLES and proceed G.6.6.5.7 West outskirts DUNKIRK	W.M.M.
	23rd to 30th		Unit employed on Camp and D. O.R.E.	W.M.M.
	30th		O.C. proceeds to PERONNE.	

W.H. Miller Lt R.E.
a/o/c 470 Field Coy

Army Form C. 2118.

WAR DIARY
or
INTELLIGENCE SUMMARY.   470 FIELD COY
MAY 1919
(Erase heading not required.)

Instructions regarding War Diaries and Intelligence Summaries are contained in F.S. Regs., Part II., and the Staff Manual respectively. Title pages will be prepared in manuscript.

Hour, Date, Place	Summary of Events and Information	Remarks and references to Appendices
DUNKIRK 1st to 31st	Unit engaged on checking and preparing Cadre equipment ready for embarkation to U.K. Available men employed by D.O.R.E. of district in L. of C. areas.	9/5/ 28 {WHM}

W H Miller Lt RE
a/o/c 470 Field Coy

[Stamp: 470th (NORTH MIDLAND) FIELD COY. R.E. Date ...]

Army Form C. 2118.

WAR DIARY
or
INTELLIGENCE SUMMARY

470 FIELD COY
JUNE 1919

(Erase heading not required.)

Instructions regarding War Diaries and Intelligence Summaries are contained in F. S. Regs., Part II. and the Staff Manual respectively. Title Pages will be prepared in manuscript.

Place	Date	Hour	Summary of Events and Information	Remarks and references to Appendices
MARDYCK CAMP DUNKIRK	1st	1st-6th	The Cadre of this unit was further reduced to one Officer and along no other ranks. The Cadre of this unit was employed in preparing the stores and equipment of unit in readiness for embarkation to U.K. also general camp duties in their camp at MARDYCKE, ST POL, DUNKIRK.	W.O.M.M.
"	7th		Orders received to divide Cadre into two parts a) Equipment Guard b) Official Cadre to proceed straightway to U.K. Eighteen men were despatched as Cadre reducing personnel down to 1 Officer & 13 o.R. forming "Equipment Guard."	W.O.M.M.
"	7-17th		"Equipment Guard" employed on guarding vehicles and equipment.	3 W.O.M.M.
"	18-30th		Equipment Guard employed in painting and numbering vehicles and packages as per instructions received from D.A.G. code.	5 W.O.M.M.

Date 30-6-19
470 (North Midland) Field Coy R.E.

3 - JUL 1919
OFFICE RECORD SECTION, WINCHESTER

Commander R.E.
a/b/c. 470 FIELD COY
R.E.

WAR DIARY or INTELLIGENCE SUMMARY

Army Form C. 2118.

JULY 19

447D FIELD COY R.E.

Place	Date	Hour	Summary of Events and Information	Remarks and references to Appendices
DUNKIRK	1st to 8th	9 a	Equipment guard employed on stores and equipment.	WDM
"		9 am	Orders received for equipment guard to proceed to U.K.	WDM
		10 am	Vehicles and stores moved from camp down to Dunkirk Docks.	WDM
	12th to 15th		Vehicles and stores loaded and despatched in barges and stores lists signed for by S.E.s Chatham Railway Coy	WDM
	16th		Equipment guard proceeds to Boulogne for dispersal	WDM

Final Entry
WATM

Signed WATMules Lt RE
16-7-19
O.C.

www.ingramcontent.com/pod-product-compliance
Lightning Source LLC
Chambersburg PA
CBHW081458160426
43193CB00013B/2528